NEW YORK Mets IQ

THE ULTIMATE TEST OF TRUE FANDOM

Copyright © 2019 Tucker Elliot.

All rights reserved.

ISBN: 978-1-7343585-0-6

Special thanks to Dan "One Win" Monfre.

Front cover photo courtesy of Chris Camino.

Interior layout and formatting by BMP Digital.

Black Mesa

Florida

CONTENTS

	INTRODUCTION	i
1	THE NUMBERS GAME	1
2	BASEBALL QUOTES	13
3	FRANCHISE LEADERS	23
4	OCTOBER BASEBALL	33
5	FANTASTIC FEATS	45
6	AWARD WINNERS	55
7	THE HITTERS	67
8	THE PITCHERS	79
9	THE TEAMS	91
10	EXTRA INNINGS	103

A note to readers: This book was written after the 2019 regular season concluded. All stats and references to "franchise record" or "only player in Mets history" or "MLB record" are accurate for the years 1962-2019.

For John Abrams
Diehard fan since 1962
And the best "water cooler" colleague in the business

INTRODUCTION

Arthur Daley, the Pulitzer Prize-winning sportswriter for the *New York Times*, wrote more than eleven thousand daily columns and twenty million words covering sports all over the world—but his favorite sport was baseball, and on that subject he famously wrote, "A baseball fan has the digestive apparatus of a billy goat. He can, and does, devour any set of statistics with insatiable appetite and then nuzzles hungrily for more."

Daley was right, of course.

Baseball relies on numbers and statistics more than any other sport—and we use those numbers to measure success and failure, they guide our decisions in playing and managing the game, they fuel our discussions when watching the game as a spectator or reliving it over the water cooler at work, and they keep us awake late at night, celebrating or lamenting, depending on, well, the final score.

Numbers, for the most part, don't lie.

Statistics on the other hand ... well, it depends who you ask.

Bob Woolf was a Boston lawyer and a pioneer in the business of representing athletes in contract negotiations and sponsorship deals. In other words, he was one of the first sports agents. Woolf related this anecdote about Boston Red Sox pitcher Bob Stanley: "When I negotiated his contract with the Red Sox, we had statistics demonstrating he was the third best pitcher in the league. They had a chart showing he was the sixtieth best pitcher in the Red Sox organization." Perhaps it's the ability to manipulate and interpret statistics that makes numbers so fascinating to baseball fans.

Here's what I know about baseball and numbers that is incontrovertible: Math was my favorite grade school subject because it was the easiest. I knew it already from calculating batting averages and earned run averages and projecting how many hits and RBIs I'd have at the end of the season based on the games I'd already played—math skills that were easily three or four years ahead of my grade level at the time. My mom was the official scorekeeper at our Little League games and we'd spend hours each week pouring through the scorebook, tabulating all the stats, and then placing them in columns and charts on construction paper as if it was the back of my very own Topps baseball card.

Numbers resonate with baseball fans, no question about it.

It's not just the stats, either. We use numbers to track the performance of our favorite players, sure, but we also use numbers to identify them—as in jersey numbers. I met Johnny Bench once during spring training. Big surprise—I wore #5 a few weeks later when my summer league kicked off. You can track my idols using my Little League and high school jersey numbers: #5 (Bench), #8 (Gary Carter), #23 (Don Mattingly), and #8 again (Cal Ripken Jr.). There's a very good reason why franchises retire jersey numbers to honor their most important stars—just as a fan wearing a #20 Mets jersey is making a statement about Pete Alonso's contributions to the club, when the club retires a number it's making a statement about that player's significance to the history of the entire organization.

This is a book of trivia, but it is derived from numbers.

And collectively they tell the story of the New York Mets.

Now step up to the plate.

Challenge yourself.

Enjoy, and reminisce.

This is your New York Mets IQ, the ultimate test of true fandom.

"My father's faith in me, often greater than my own, is the single most important factor of me being inducted into this Hall of Fame."

Mike Piazza

1 THE NUMBERS GAME

Any self-respecting fan should be able to cite the most notable and historic stats in franchise history—and you should also be able to identify the most revered jersey numbers as well. Mets history is replete with superstars and individuals who distinguished themselves as fan-favorites, and that's why we open the top of the first with a simple numbers game: Do you know the jersey numbers for these all-time greats?

TOP OF THE FIRST

Q1: Mike Piazza was a seven-time All-Star in New York—and his 396 career home runs are the most in major-league history by a catcher (he hit 427 total HRs). He was elected to the Hall of Fame in 2016, the same year the Mets retired his jersey number in a ceremony at Citi Field. What number did Piazza wear for the Mets?
- a) 13
- b) 31
- c) 25
- d) 33

Q2: Tom Seaver won 311 major-league games in a career that spanned 20 seasons—but he did his best work for the Mets. Seaver was a nine-time All-Star in New York, a World Series champion, and a perennial Cy Young candidate. The Mets retired Seaver's jersey number in 1988, and he was inducted into the Hall of Fame in 1992. What number did Seaver wear for the Mets?
- a) 14
- b) 24
- c) 41
- d) 42

Q3: Gil Hodges hit the first home run in Mets history on April 11, 1962. However, his jersey number was retired in 1973 because he managed the Miracle Mets to victory in the 1969 World Series. What number did Hodges wear as manager of the Mets?
- a) 14
- b) 17
- c) 20
- d) 23

Q4: Hall of Fame legend Casey Stengel was the first manager in Mets history. The Mets retired his jersey number in 1965, and he was inducted into the Mets Hall of Fame in 1981. What number did Stengel wear as manager of the Mets?
- a) 7
- b) 17
- c) 27
- d) 37

Q5: David Wright earned the nickname "Captain America" when he was the captain for Team USA in the 2013 World Baseball Classic. Wright was a first-round draft pick in 2001, and he was the face of the franchise for more than a decade. He spent his entire career in a Mets uniform, and his name is at or near the top of numerous franchise leaderboards. What jersey number did the seven-time All-Star wear for the Mets?
- a) 5
- b) 15
- c) 20
- d) 25

Q6: The Mets selected Dwight Gooden out of Hillsborough High School in Tampa, Florida, with the overall fifth pick in the first-round of the 1982 Amateur Draft. Less than two years later, the 19-year-old phenom took baseball by storm. What jersey number did Gooden wear for the Mets?
- a) 11
- b) 13
- c) 16
- d) 17

Q7: Jerry Koosman signed with the Mets in 1964, after a scout saw

him pitching for an army team at Fort Bliss in Texas. The Minnesota native won two pennants and a World Series ring during 12 seasons pitching for the Mets. As the franchise celebrated the 50th anniversary of the Miracle Mets in 2019, it was announced that the club would retire Koosman's jersey number in 2020. Koosman said, "To know that my number will be retired and sit alongside other team legends is one of the greatest tributes I could ever be granted. I was always proud to be a Met. Today, I am even prouder." What jersey number did Koosman wear for the Mets?
    a) 27
    b) 47
    c) 36
    d) 24

Q8: The Mets selected Darryl Strawberry out of Crenshaw High School in Los Angeles, California, with the overall number one pick in the 1980 Amateur Draft. He debuted just three years later, and was the first player in Mets history to hit 20 or more home runs as a rookie. What jersey number did Strawberry wear for the Mets?
    a) 18
    b) 21
    c) 24
    d) 27

Q9: Jacob deGrom was a shortstop in college. He began to pitch some in relief as a junior, but really it was the influence of scout Steve Nichols that convinced the Mets to select deGrom as a pitcher in the ninth-round of the 2010 Amateur Draft. The rest, as they say, is history. What jersey number did deGrom wear for the Mets?
    a) 18
    b) 28

c) 38
d) 48

Q10: Carlos Beltran hit eight home runs for the Houston Astros in the 2004 NL playoffs—and his reward was a monster free agent contract with the Mets in the offseason. In parts of seven seasons from 2005-11, Beltran hit 149 home runs with 559 RBIs—numbers surpassed only by David Wright. What jersey number did Beltran wear for the Mets?
   a) 10
   b) 15
   c) 20
   d) 25

TOP OF THE FIRST ANSWER KEY

1: b. 31.

2: c. 41.

3: a. 14.

4: d. 37.

5: a. 5.

6: c. 16.

7: c. 36.

8: a. 18.

9: d. 48.

10: b. 15.

BOTTOM OF THE FIRST

Q11: Venezuela native Edgardo Alfonzo signed with the Mets as an amateur free agent in 1991—and by the mid-nineties he was a mainstay in the middle of the lineup. In a six-year stretch from 1997-2002, Alfonzo led the Mets with 947 hits. He also hit 112 home runs with 457 RBIs—totals that were second only to Mike Piazza. What jersey number did Alfonzo wear for the Mets?
- a) 12
- b) 11
- c) 14
- d) 13

Q12: Dominican Republic native Jose Reyes was a 19-year-old kid when he debuted with the Mets in 2003. Just two years later the switch-hitting shortstop with unbelievable speed led the league in both triples and stolen bases. Reyes would go on to hit 93 triples in seven seasons from 2005-11. That total easily led the NL in that stretch. Jimmy Rollins was second on that list with 59 triples for the Phillies. What jersey number did Reyes wear for the Mets?
- a) 3
- b) 7
- c) 13
- d) 17

Q13: The St. Louis Cardinals originally drafted Keith Hernandez in 1971 ... *in the 42nd round.* The Mets acquired Hernandez in a trade in 1983, and by that time he was a perennial winner and one of the most consistent hitters in the league. Hernandez was already a World Series champion with the Cardinals, and his veteran presence was crucial to the Mets during their 1986 championship run. What jersey

number did Hernandez wear for the Mets?
   a) 7
   b) 13
   c) 17
   d) 23

Q14: Al Leiter came to the Mets in a trade from the Florida Marlins. In seven seasons from 1998-2004, Leiter won 95 games—easily the highest total on the team in that span, and the sixth highest total in the NL. His arm was a big reason the Mets won consecutive wild-cards in 1999-2000, and the 2000 NL pennant. What jersey number did Leiter wear for the Mets?
   a) 22
   b) 23
   c) 24
   d) 25

Q15: The Mets traded pitcher Walt Terrell to the Detroit Tigers for Howard Johnson in 1984. Johnson was basically a kid at that point, but he was already a world champion with the Tigers and had a powerful bat from either side of the plate. Johnson won his second ring with the Mets in 1986, and in 1987 he began a five-year stretch in which he hit 157 home runs—second in the NL only to Darryl Strawberry. What jersey number did Johnson wear for the Mets?
   a) 5
   b) 4
   c) 44
   d) 20

Q16: David Cone was drafted by the Kansas City Royals in 1981, and traded to the Mets in 1987. From 1988 onward, he was a perennial Cy Young candidate. Cone won 80 games for the Mets from 1987-92, the fifth highest total in the league and second on the club only to Dwight Gooden during that span. What jersey number did Cone wear for the Mets?

- a) 13
- b) 36
- c) 44
- d) 22

Q17: Ron Darling was selected by the Texas Rangers with the ninth overall pick in the first-round of the 1981 Amateur Draft, and was traded to the Mets in 1982. He was a mainstay in the rotation by 1984, and in a six-year stretch through 1989 he won 86 games. That total was fourth highest in the league and second on the club only to Dwight Gooden during that span. What jersey number did Darling wear for the Mets?

- a) 44
- b) 12
- c) 15
- d) 17

Q18: Mets general manager Brodie Van Wagenen had this to say after Pete Alonso was named 2019 National League Rookie of the Year: "Pete kept the same attitude that he came into Spring Training with through the entire season. He was a good teammate. He was a true professional. And obviously, he was lightning in a bottle for all Mets fans." What jersey number did Alonso wear during his record-setting rookie season?

- a) 15
- b) 20
- c) 25
- d) 30

Q19: Dominican Republic native Amed Rosario was a 16-year-old kid when he signed with the Mets as an amateur free agent in 2012. By 2017, MLBPipeline.com ranked Rosario as the No. 2 prospect in baseball—and ESPN's Keith Law said, "He has MVP potential." Later that summer he made his big league debut, and it turns out the hype was real. In his first two-plus seasons with the Mets, Rosario had 360 base hits—more than any other player on the club during that stretch. What jersey number did Rosario wear for the Mets?
   a) 1
   b) 2
   c) 3
   d) 4

Q20: The Mets selected Michael Conforto out of Oregon State University with the overall tenth pick in the first-round of the 2014 Amateur Draft. He made his big league debut in 2015, and in his second game he was 4-for-4 with two doubles and four runs scored. A day later he became just the second player in Mets history to drive home at least one run in his first three career games. In parts of five seasons from 2015-19, Conforto had 491 hits—more than any other player on the club during that stretch. What jersey number did Conforto wear for the Mets?
   a) 3
   b) 13
   c) 23
   d) 30

BOTTOM OF THE FIRST ANSWER KEY

11: d. 13.

12: b. 7.

13: c. 17.

14: a. 22.

15: d. 20.

16: c. 44.

17: b. 12.

18: b. 20.

19: a. 1.

20: d. 30.

"A good professional athlete must have the love of a little boy, and the good players feel the kind of love for the game that they did when they were little leaguers."

Tom Seaver

2 BASEBALL QUOTES

No other sport inspires quotes like baseball. Dozens of books are out there filled with nothing but quotes from the game's great players, managers, umpires, writers, and broadcasters. One reason we're fascinated with baseball quotes is because they tell us the history of the game in the words of those who were there to make or witness firsthand the plays that inspired generations of fans. And lucky for us, baseball has inspired more written words than any other sport.

Here in the second our trivia is inspired by our love for baseball quotes. Do you know who said these words? Or, do you know which players these words were spoken about?

TOP OF THE SECOND

Q21: Cleon Jones, an outfielder who caught the final out of the 1969 World Series, made it clear who he thought deserved credit for the victory: "Everybody I've talked to says he's the guy who made the difference between being world champions and a second-rate ball club. We would have been real happy to finish second. But he wasn't satisfied with that."
    a) Tom Seaver
    b) Tommie Agee
    c) Gil Hodges
    d) Jerry Koosman

Q22: Jerry Crasnick wrote about this player: "Low on drama and high in results … when an athlete is so unassuming and mind-numbingly consistent, it's easy to lose track or sell him short."
    a) John Olerud
    b) Carlos Beltran
    c) David Wright
    d) Cliff Floyd

Q23: In his best-selling book, this member of the 1986 world champion Mets (rightfully) referred to teammate Lenny Dykstra as "one of baseball's all-time thugs."
    a) Keith Hernandez
    b) Darryl Strawberry
    c) Dwight Gooden
    d) Ron Darling

Q24: Mets manager Davey Johnson said of this player: "He's a horse. He's in great shape. You try to rest him during the season, but he

won't stand for it.
   a) Gary Carter
   b) Ray Knight
   c) Kevin Mitchell
   d) Howard Johnson

Q25: Baseball legend Hank Aaron famously said of this player: "Kid, I know who you are, and before your career is over, I guarantee you everyone in this stadium will, too."
   a) Nolan Ryan
   b) Tom Seaver
   c) Dwight Gooden
   d) Jacob deGrom

Q26: This pitcher shared his simplistic—and effective—approach to the game: "My goal is to put up zeroes. You feel like you do that, you put your team in a pretty good position to win."
   a) Nolan Ryan
   b) Tom Seaver
   c) Dwight Gooden
   d) Jacob deGrom

Q27: This pitcher had the talent to back up these words: "I don't talk. I just let what I do talk for myself."
   a) Dwight Gooden
   b) David Cone
   c) Sid Fernandez
   d) Johan Santana

Q28: Joan Hodges, widow of former Mets manager Gil Hodges, had heartfelt words about this player: "He made believers out of all of us."
   a) Tug McGraw

b) Tom Seaver
c) Jerry Koosman
d) Ron Swoboda

Q29: This pitcher said: "It was a different time. We didn't have pitch counts. We didn't lift weights or take any supplements. But I grew up on a farm and had a strong body. I just got used to throwing 130 pitches a game, and I hated coming out of games."
a) Tom Seaver
b) Jerry Koosman
c) Gary Gentry
d) Don Cardwell

Q30: This player waxed philosophical when reflecting on his career: "The gift I had as a baseball player didn't make me a man. It just made me a baseball player. I had to take off the uniform to become a man. Most celebrities can't remove the uniform. They can't remove the film or the music or whatever made them famous. That's why they end up going down this road. When you keep chasing old memories of who you used to be, you can never become who you can be."
a) Wally Backman
b) Lenny Dykstra
c) Dwight Gooden
d) Darryl Strawberry

TOP OF THE SECOND ANSWER KEY

21: c. Gil Hodges.

22: b. Carlos Beltran.

23: d. Ron Darling (*108 Stitches*).

24: a. Gary Carter.

25: b. Tom Seaver.

26: d. Jacob deGrom.

27: d. Johan Santana.

28: a. Tug McGraw.

29: b. Jerry Koosman.

30: d. Darryl Strawberry.

BOTTOM OF THE SECOND

Q31: This player said: "Getting to New York … was truly one of the greatest blessings of my life. When I first got there it wasn't the easiest introduction … but then once I decided to really become a Met and embrace the city, things changed for me, and for the better."
  a) Tom Glavine
  b) Keith Hernandez
  c) Mike Piazza
  d) Gary Carter

Q32: At the end of his career, this player said: "As far as regrets go, I can't say I have any. I knew one way to play the game."
  a) Mike Piazza
  b) Johan Santana
  c) John Olerud
  d) David Wright

Q33: This player reminisced about the 1986 World Series title: "We fulfilled our dream … it takes 25 to win. Five coaches, one manager, GM and front office. Seven months counting spring training. Every team comes in with one goal. To be a world champion. Only one comes out to be that. I was very fortunate. A very, very gratifying team feeling."
  a) Mookie Wilson
  b) Tim Teufel
  c) Keith Hernandez
  d) Gary Carter

Q34: This player reflected on his career: "I miss the challenge, the competition, the trying to get your swing right and get in a zone …

and the camaraderie … [but] I don't miss the slumps."
a) Howard Johnson
b) John Olerud
c) Ike Davis
d) Mike Piazza

Q35: This pitcher said: "In high school, all I had to do was throw hard. In the minors, all I had to do was throw hard strikes. In the majors, though, you have to spot your pitches—and that's hard work."
a) David Cone
b) Dwight Gooden
c) Sid Fernandez
d) Jacob deGrom

Q36: This player credited his mental approach to former pitcher Frank Viola: "I like to maintain a positive attitude and just kind of take a deep breath and step back from things. [He] was a huge help, because he really got me to understand that baseball is a game and I need to go out there and have fun with it."
a) Noah Syndergaard
b) Jacob deGrom
c) Matt Harvey
d) Jeurys Familia

Q37: This world champion reflected on 1986: "We didn't have anything going on in the early '80s, took our licks the first few years. But it was great, very memorable, to go from the worst to the best."
a) Roger McDowell
b) Jesse Orosco
c) Randy Niemann
d) Doug Sisk

Q38: Upon finding out he would be inducted into the New York Mets Hall of Fame, this player said: "You can't judge a person by his size, but you could judge him by the heart he has—and I have always had a big heart. Every time I went out there I gave 150 percent."
   a) Mookie Wilson
   b) Bud Harrelson
   c) Tug McGraw
   d) John Franco

Q39: Long-time umpire Durwood Merrill wrote a book titled *You're Out and You're Ugly, Too*. In his book, Merrill called this pitcher a "junkyard dog" because "he'll knock you out of the box without blinking."
   a) Tom Seaver
   b) David Cone
   c) Bobby Jones
   d) Dwight Gooden

Q40: Former GM Sandy Alderson admitted he wished he could "have that one back" when asked about letting this player leave New York as a free agent. He added, "He's a very good player, an excellent offensive player … I applaud him for what he's done."
   a) Lucas Duda
   b) Daniel Murphy
   c) Wilmer Flores
   d) Travis d'Arnaud

BOTTOM OF THE SECOND ANSWER KEY

31: c. Mike Piazza.

32: d. David Wright.

33: c. Keith Hernandez.

34: b. John Olerud.

35: b. Dwight Gooden.

36: a. Noah Syndergaard.

37: b. Jesse Orosco.

38: d. John Franco.

39: b. David Cone.

40: b. Daniel Murphy.

"I live and die with this team. I think that's what made the connection between the fans and me so strong."

David Wright

3 FRANCHISE LEADERS

It's impossible to tell the story of major-league baseball without the Mets ... because so much of baseball history was made by this beloved franchise. The record books are filled with guys who called Shea Stadium "home" and meant it as more than just a park.

Regular season. Postseason. It doesn't matter.

The biggest names in baseball.

Here in the third, we explore some of the most significant franchise records and relive moments from some of the biggest names in the game.

TOP OF THE THIRD

Q41: This player set a franchise record with 227 hits in a single-season—a total that also ranks among the top five in the NL since the Mets began play in 1962. Who owns this franchise record?
  a) Jose Reyes
  b) Lance Johnson
  c) David Wright
  d) Edgardo Alfonzo

Q42: Cleon Jones hit a franchise record .340 for the 1969 Miracle Mets. That record lasted four decades until it was finally surpassed by two players in the same season. Who set a new franchise record with a .354 average?
  a) Mike Piazza
  b) John Olerud
  c) Moises Alou
  d) Lance Johnson

Q43: Only one player in franchise history slugged .600 for an entire season. Who holds this record?
  a) Mike Piazza
  b) Bobby Bonilla
  c) Carlos Beltran
  d) Pete Alonso

Q44: In February 2019, former GM Sandy Alderson was asked about the future of the Mets. In his reply, he said, "There are guys that are close, like Pete Alonso, that I want to follow." Well, he got that one right. Alonso shattered records all season long. He hit 53 home runs. No one in Mets history had ever hit 50—and only three players had hit 40, and none of them were rookies. The previous single-season home run record was 41. Which two players shared this record until Alonso came along?

    a) Darryl Strawberry/Mike Piazza
    b) Todd Hundley/Carlos Beltran
    c) Carlos Delgado/Howard Johnson
    d) Dave Kingman/Cliff Floyd

Q45: And a follow-up ... it's not often that a record measured by simply counting events is *doubled*. But Alonso did that, plus one. The Mets previous single-season home run record for rookies was 26. Who held this previous record?

    a) Jay Payton
    b) Ron Swoboda
    c) Ike Davis
    d) Darryl Strawberry

Q46: Only nine players had 1,000 career hits for the Mets. Who set a franchise record with 1,777 base hits?

    a) Cleon Jones
    b) Edgardo Alfonzo
    c) Jose Reyes
    d) David Wright

Q47: Only three players hit 200 home runs for the Mets. Who hit a franchise record 252 big flies?

    a) David Wright
    b) Mike Piazza
    c) Darryl Strawberry
    d) Howard Johnson

Q48: This catcher was the first player in Mets history to hit 40 home runs in a single-season—and his 41 total home runs set a major-league record for catchers that has been surpassed just once, by Javy Lopez for the Atlanta Braves in 2003. Who achieved this powerful feat?

a) John Buck
b) John Stearns
c) Mike Piazza
d) Todd Hundley

Q49: The franchise record for games played is an astounding 1,853. Only ten players have surpassed 1,000 games—and only two played more than 1,500. Who played a record 1,853 games for the Mets?

a) Bud Harrelson
b) Jose Reyes
c) David Wright
d) Ed Kranepool

Q50: The Mets single-season record for shutouts is eight. It's hard to imagine anyone breaking this record, given the emphasis on pitch counts in today's game. Whose name is in the record books for this feat?

a) Dwight Gooden
b) Tom Seaver
c) Jerry Koosman
d) David Cone

TOP OF THE THIRD ANSWER KEY

41: b. Lance Johnson (1996).

42: b. John Olerud (1998; Mike Piazza hit .348 that same year).

43: a. Mike Piazza (he did it twice: .607 in 1998, and .614 in 2000).

44: b. Todd Hundley (1996)/Carlos Beltran (2006).

45: d. Darryl Strawberry (1983).

46: d. David Wright.

47: c. Darryl Strawberry.

48: d. Todd Hundley.

49: d. Ed Kranepool (1962-79).

50: a. Dwight Gooden (1985).

BOTTOM OF THE THIRD

Q51: This manager won 595 regular season games—a franchise record. Who is the winningest manager in Mets history?
 a) Terry Collins
 b) Bobby Valentine
 c) Davey Johnson
 d) Gil Hodges

Q52: This pitcher set franchise records with 695 appearances and 276 saves. Who holds these records?
 a) Armando Benitez
 b) Jesse Orosco
 c) John Franco
 d) Roger McDowell

Q53: Tom Seaver set a franchise record when he struck out 19 batters in a 2-1 victory vs. the San Diego Padres on April 22, 1970. Who was the second pitcher in Mets history with 19 strikeouts in a single-game?
 a) Dwight Gooden
 b) Sid Fernandez
 c) David Cone
 d) Nolan Ryan

Q54: This pitcher had a franchise record five career games with 15-plus strikeouts. Who achieved this extraordinary feat?
 a) Tom Seaver
 b) Dwight Gooden
 c) Nolan Ryan
 d) David Cone

Q55: This pitcher was the first in franchise history with 16 strikeouts and zero walks in a single-game ... and five days later, he did it again. He is the only player in major-league history—in any league, for any team—with 16 strikeouts and zero walks in consecutive starts. Who performed this historic feat for the Mets?
   a) Tom Seaver
   b) Dwight Gooden
   c) David Cone
   d) Nolan Ryan

Q56: Offensive Winning Percentage is a metric that reflects "the percentage of games a team with nine of this player would win" (Baseball-Reference.com)—assuming average pitching and defense, and requiring a minimum of 1,500 plate appearances. If you apply this metric across all seasons of Mets history ... you get one player who, if you could suit up nine of him for every game, the Mets would be predicted to attain a .706 winning percentage. Who is this player?
   a) Mike Piazza
   b) John Olerud
   c) Howard Johnson
   d) Darryl Strawberry

Q57: The new metrics used in today's game—such as the above mentioned Offensive Winning Percentage—provide different perspectives and greater understanding of how players past and present made an impact on the game. However, in some instances, the new metrics merely reaffirm what our longstanding stats were already telling us. For example, among players with at least 1,500 plate appearances for the Mets ... whose .926 on-base plus slugging percentage (OPS) is the highest career mark in franchise history?
   a) Mike Piazza

b) John Olerud
c) Howard Johnson
d) Darryl Strawberry

Q58: Weighted On-Base Average (wOBA) was developed by Tom Tango (*The Book: Playing the Percentages in Baseball*), and is used to measure overall offensive value using the relative values of distinct offensive events (FanGraphs.com). In short, it means a traditional stat such as batting average weights all hits equally, while slugging percentage weights hits based on total bases, as if a double is twice as valuable as a single. The point of wOBA is to weight all aspects of hitting in proportion to their actual run value. FanGraphs, as a general rule for wOBA, considers .400 excellent while .320 is average. Who holds the Mets career record with a .405 wOBA?
a) Mike Piazza
b) John Olerud
c) Howard Johnson
d) Darryl Strawberry

Q59: And a follow-up … who led the 2019 Mets with a .385 wOBA?
a) J.D. Davis
b) Pete Alonso
c) Michael Conforto
d) Jeff McNeil

Q60: The franchise record for complete games in a single-season is 21. Whose name is in the record books for this historic feat?
a) Dwight Gooden
b) Tom Seaver
c) Jerry Koosman
d) David Cone

BOTTOM OF THE THIRD ANSWER KEY

51: c. Davey Johnson (1984-90).

52: c. John Franco.

53: c. David Cone (1991).

54: a. Tom Seaver.

55: b. Dwight Gooden (1984).

56: b. John Olerud.

57: b. John Olerud.

58: b. John Olerud.

59: d. Jeff McNeil.

60: b. Tom Seaver (1971).

"You work hard enough, you get the breaks and work as a team, you can become world champions."

Tom Seaver

4 OCTOBER BASEBALL

"Next year" is the mentality that 29 of baseball's 30 teams cling to each winter, for there can be only one winner—as the 1973, 2000, and 2015 clubs are painfully aware. All three won the pennant, and all three spent the offseason counting the days until spring.

In the spring, the wins column is reset.

Last season is history.

And the goal is the same for every club: October baseball.

The journey is 162 games long, and the destination is a chance for baseball immortality. Let's take a look at the Mets in the playoffs.

TOP OF THE FOURTH

Q61: Gary Gentry took the loss, 8-2, to the Houston Astros on August 13, 1969. That loss dropped the Mets into third place in the division—behind the Chicago Cubs and St. Louis Cardinals—and gave the club a season-high deficit to overcome. By how many games did the Mets trail the Cubs on that date?
　a) 8
　b) 9
　c) 10
　d) 11

Q62: Fast-forward to September 10, 1969 … the Mets swept a doubleheader vs. the Montreal Expos to move into first place for the first time in franchise history—in the NL East or otherwise, as 1969 was also the first year of divisional play. And just two weeks later, Gary Gentry shutout St. Louis, 6-0, to clinch the division. Against which team did the Mets play in the first-ever playoff game in franchise history?
　a) Cincinnati Reds
　b) Atlanta Braves
　c) Houston Astros
　d) Los Angeles Dodgers

Q63: The Mets began the best-of-five 1969 NLCS on the road. Tom Seaver got the win in Game One, despite giving up five earned runs. In fact, Seaver was the only starting pitcher to win a game in the series, as the two offenses erupted to score a combined 42 runs. Game Three was the first-ever playoff game at Shea Stadium—and as it turned out, it was the first-ever series-clinching game in franchise history as well. Who pitched seven innings of three-hit relief to get the victory as the Mets swept the NL pennant?

a) Jerry Koosman
b) Don Cardwell
c) Nolan Ryan
d) Tug McGraw

Q64: The Baltimore Orioles dominated the American League in 1969. The O's won 109 games in the regular season, and swept the Minnesota Twins in the ALCS. Game One of the 1969 World Series was in Baltimore, and the Orioles won it, 4-1. But if the home crowd thought the Orioles were going to steamroll their way to a World Series title, well ... the Mets had other plans. Jerry Koosman pitched 8 2/3 innings of two-hit ball in Game Two—and the Mets won it in the ninth, 2-1, on three consecutive two-out singles. Whose base hit made the Mets winners of a World Series game for the first time in franchise history?

a) Ron Swoboda
b) Ed Charles
c) Jerry Grote
d) Al Weis

Q65: The 1969 World Series shifted to Shea Stadium for Game Three. In that pivotal contest, Gary Gentry and Nolan Ryan combined to shutout the Orioles on four hits. Gentry even hit a two-run double against future Hall of Famer Jim Palmer. The final score, 5-0. The other star of that game made "two circus catches" (MLB.com) to back Gentry and Ryan on the mound, and for good measure, he also gave the Mets an early lead with a first-inning home run. Who was the star of Game Three of the 1969 World Series?

a) Cleon Jones
b) Art Shamsky

c) Tommie Agee
d) Ed Kranepool

Q66: Tom Seaver dominated Game Four of the 1969 World Series. Seaver carried a shutout into the ninth, but the offense had only managed a single run against O's starter Mike Cuellar—and when Frank Robinson and Boog Powell hit consecutive singles in the top of the ninth, the tying run was at third with one out … and the stage was set for "The Catch." It is perhaps the most significant defensive play in Mets history. Brooks Robinson hit a sinking line drive to right-centerfield that had no business being caught. But it *was* caught, and instead of a go-ahead, two-run extra-base hit, it was a sacrifice fly that left the game tied and gave the Mets a chance to walk-off. Who made this historic defensive play?
   a) Ron Swoboda
   b) Tommie Agee
   c) Cleon Jones
   d) Art Shamsky

Q67: And a follow-up … despite giving up the tying run in the ninth, Tom Seaver took the mound in the tenth inning and hung another zero on the board. The Mets won in the bottom of the tenth, 2-1, when a throwing error by pitcher Pete Richert on a sacrifice bunt allowed pinch-runner Rod Gaspar to score from second base. Only one other pitcher in Mets history had a 10-inning complete game in the postseason. Who pitched 10 innings to beat the Houston Astros, 2-1, in Game Five of the 1986 NLCS?
   a) Ron Darling
   b) Dwight Gooden
   c) Bob Ojeda
   d) Sid Fernandez

Q68: The Baltimore Orioles hit 172 home runs in 1969—the third highest total in the AL—while the Mets hit just 109, which was only eighth out of 12 teams in the NL. But in the 1969 World Series, the Mets out-homered the Orioles 6-3. Who hit three home runs for the Mets and was named MVP of the 1969 World Series?
  a) Cleon Jones
  b) Tommie Agee
  c) Donn Clendenon
  d) Ed Kranepool

Q69: In Game Five of the 1969 World Series, Orioles pitcher Dave McNally hit a two-run home run in the third inning … and two outs later, Frank Robinson hit a solo home run to give Baltimore a 3-0 lead. And yet … this pitcher hung in there, and tossed a complete game. The Mets rallied to win, 5-3. Who was on the mound to close out the 1969 World Series?
  a) Jerry Koosman
  b) Gary Gentry
  c) Nolan Ryan
  d) Ron Taylor

Q70: There's some irony here … who made the last out of the 1969 World Series?
  a) Frank Robinson
  b) Boog Powell
  c) Brooks Robinson
  d) Davey Johnson

TOP OF THE FOURTH ANSWER KEY

61: c. 10.

62: b. Atlanta Braves.

63: c. Nolan Ryan.

64: d. Al Weis.

65: c. Tommie Agee.

66: a. Ron Swoboda.

67: b. Dwight Gooden.

68: c. Donn Clendenon.

69: a. Jerry Koosman.

70: d. Davey Johnson (he would later manage the Mets to victory in the 1986 World Series).

BOTTOM OF THE FOURTH

Q71: The Mets won seven straight and 11 of 13 in a torrid September playoff chase in 1973. The club was in fourth place, 2.5 games back of the Pirates—and trailing the Expos and Cardinals as well—but rallied to take a 1.5 game lead into the final series of the season. The Mets clinched the NL East on the season's final day, despite winning just 82 games. The Cincinnati Reds won 99 games and the NL West, and were heavily favored in the NLCS. In Game Three, with the series tied 1-1 and emotions on hyper-drive ... whose confrontation with Pete Rose led to a postseason bench-clearing brawl between the Mets and the Reds?
 a) Bud Harrelson
 b) Jerry Koosman
 c) Cleon Jones
 d) Jerry Grote

Q72: The Mets won Game Three of the 1973 NLCS, 9-2, and had a chance to win the pennant the following day. However, a seventh-inning homer by Tony Perez tied the game, 1-1, and then Pete Rose won it with an extra-inning home run in the 12th. But Game Five was never in doubt. Early runs plus dominant pitching gave the Mets a second improbable pennant in five years. Who was on the mound to close out the 7-2 victory vs. the Reds?
 a) Tom Seaver
 b) Jerry Koosman
 c) Harry Parker
 d) Tug McGraw

Q73: In the 1973 NLCS vs. Cincinnati, this pitcher tossed a two-hitter for the first postseason complete game shutout in Mets history.

Who achieved this extraordinary feat?
a) Jon Matlack
b) Gary Gentry
c) Jerry Koosman
d) Jim McAndrew

Q74: And a follow-up … who is the only pitcher in Mets history to throw a one-hit shutout in the playoffs?
a) Tom Seaver
b) David Cone
c) Mike Hampton
d) Bobby Jones

Q75: Tom Seaver set a franchise postseason record when he struck out 13 batters in Game One of the 1973 NLCS vs. Cincinnati. Who tied this record with 13 strikeouts in a playoff game vs. the Los Angeles Dodgers?
a) Dwight Gooden
b) Noah Syndergaard
c) Jacob deGrom
d) David Cone

Q76: Tommie Agee hit the first-ever playoff home run in Mets history during Game Two of the 1969 NLCS vs. the Atlanta Braves. Who hit a franchise record seven postseason home runs?
a) Daniel Murphy
b) Mike Piazza
c) Rusty Staub
d) Darryl Strawberry

Q77: The 1986 NLCS between the Mets and Astros is widely considered to be among the most compelling playoff series in major-

league history. In Game Five, with the series tied two games apiece, the Mets had just two hits through 11 innings … but with two hits in the 12th, the club won a dramatic walk-off, 2-1. Whose base hit won Game Five of the 1986 NLCS?
a) Lenny Dykstra
b) Keith Hernandez
c) Gary Carter
d) Ray Knight

Q78: Game Six of the 1986 NLCS was a 16-inning marathon on the road in Houston. The Astros scored three runs in the first, and the Mets tied it with three runs in the ninth. Both teams scored a run in the 14th. The Mets scored three runs in the 16th, and then withstood a final assault by the Astros' offense in the bottom of the frame. The Mets somehow prevailed, 7-6, to claim the NL pennant. Houston lost the series, but Mike Scott was so dominant on the mound for the Astros that he won Series MVP honors. But this guy got the win in Game Six, and he was on the mound to clinch the pennant … and he was also the first player in NLCS history to win three games out of the bullpen in a single-series. Who beat the Astros three times out of the bullpen in the 1986 NLCS?
a) Roger McDowell
b) Rick Aguilera
c) Jesse Orosco
d) Doug Sisk

Q79: The 1986 ALCS was similarly epic. The California Angels were a strike away from the pennant in Game Five, but Boston's Dave Henderson hit a game-tying home run to send the game into extra-innings. The Red Sox won, 7-6, in 11 innings to send the series back to Boston—and the Angels never recovered, as the Red Sox handily won Games Six and Seven to set up a showdown with the Mets in the World Series. The road team won the first four games of the 1986 World Series, which meant the Mets faced elimination in Game Six. And when the Mets were down two runs in the 10th, and down to their last out, this Red Sox pitcher was prematurely selected as World Series MVP. But then: Gary Carter singled, Kevin Mitchell singled, Ray Knight singled to score Carter, a wild pitch scored Mitchell, and then Mookie Wilson hit a ground ball to Bill Buckner at first. It was a routine play, until it wasn't. Buckner's infamous error scored Knight, and forced a Game Seven. Which Red Sox pitcher was "MVP" of the 1986 World Series?

a) Roger Clemens
b) Bruce Hurst
c) Calvin Schiraldi
d) Al Nipper

Q80: And a follow-up … the Red Sox scored three early runs in Game Seven, but the Mets rallied for three in the sixth—and then the *actual* Series MVP hit a home run in the seventh to put the Mets ahead, 4-3. New York would hold on, 8-5, for the second World Series title in franchise history. Who was MVP of the 1986 World Series?

a) Gary Carter
b) Kevin Mitchell
c) Ray Knight
d) Mookie Wilson

BOTTOM OF THE FOURTH ANSWER KEY

71: a. Bud Harrelson.

72: d. Tug McGraw.

73: a. Jon Matlack.

74: d. Bobby Jones (2000 NLDS vs. San Francisco).

75: c. Jacob deGrom (2015).

76: a. Daniel Murphy.

77: c. Gary Carter.

78: c. Jesse Orosco.

79: b. Bruce Hurst.

80: c. Ray Knight.

"Every experience that I've had, it's just all led up to the success and the joy of this year. I'm just so happy that everything has come together the way it has, and I'm just looking to try and be even better next year, and win more games, get to the playoffs and win a championship."

Pete Alonso

5 FANTASTIC FEATS

Fantastic feats are what draw us to the water cooler at work on Monday morning. "Did you see …?" is how the conversation begins. And inevitably it leads to stories about other guys, and more ridiculously impressive feats. Some fantastic feats are best told through numbers. Some defy any explanation at all. But all are worth sharing. For example: *Did you see Pete Alonso in the Home Run Derby last night?*

You see how that works?

Here in the fifth, it's all about the fantastic feats.

TOP OF THE FIFTH

Q81: Only one player in Mets history has ever hit safely in 30 consecutive games. Who achieved this fantastic feat?
   a) David Wright
   b) John Olerud
   c) Mike Piazza
   d) Moises Alou

Q82: The longest postseason hitting streak in Mets history is 13 games. Two players achieved this feat—and remarkably, they were teammates, and their streaks ended just two days apart in the same postseason series. Which teammates share this record?
   a) Timo Perez/Todd Zeile
   b) Darryl Strawberry/Keith Hernandez
   c) Benny Agbayani/Edgardo Alfonzo
   d) Jay Payton/Mike Piazza

Q83: This player reached base safely in a franchise record 47 consecutive games over two seasons. In that stretch, he hit .380 with nine home runs, 28 RBIs, 31 runs, 60 hits, and 46 walks. Who achieved this fantastic feat?
   a) John Olerud
   b) David Wright
   c) Carlos Delgado
   d) Carlos Beltran

Q84: This player reached base safely in 34 consecutive games during a single-season—which is also a franchise record. And he did it as a rookie. Who achieved this fantastic feat?
   a) Jose Reyes

b) David Wright
c) Pete Alonso
d) Dave Magadan

Q85: More than a dozen players in Mets history have hit home runs in four consecutive games … but only one player has ever homered in *five* consecutive games. Who achieved this fantastic feat?
a) Curtis Granderson
b) John Buck
c) Richard Hidalgo
d) Bobby Bonilla

Q86: This player had a two-week stretch in which he scored at least one run in a franchise record 13 consecutive games. He scored 15 total runs, and also had 18 hits, four doubles, three home runs, 13 RBIs, and 12 walks. The most astounding part was that his numbers went unrewarded—Willie Harris for the Nationals, and Conor Jackson for the Diamondbacks won Player of the Week honors with significantly less impressive stats. Still … who achieved this fantastic feat?
a) David Wright
b) Carlos Beltran
c) Gary Sheffield
d) Carlos Delgado

Q87: Only one player in Mets history has ever produced at least one RBI in 10 consecutive games … and he did it twice. He had a 10-game streak in August, and then the following year in June and July he had an extraordinary 15-game streak in which he had at least one RBI in every game. Who achieved this fantastic feat?
a) Edgardo Alfonzo
b) Jeff Kent

c) David Wright
d) Mike Piazza

Q88: Tommie Agee set a franchise record in 1970 when he had at least one extra-base hit in seven consecutive games. He hit three doubles and six home runs in that streak. That record stood until 2004, when Ty Wigginton had five doubles and four home runs during a streak of eight consecutive games with an extra-base hit. Who set a new franchise record when he hit at least one extra-base hit in *nine* consecutive games in 2016?
   a) Curtis Granderson
   b) Michael Conforto
   c) Neil Walker
   d) Yoenis Cespedes

Q89: Only ten players in Mets history have hit for the cycle. Jim Hickman hit the first on August 7, 1963. Whose cycle on April 27, 2012, is the most recent?
   a) Scott Hairston
   b) Daniel Murphy
   c) Ike Davis
   d) Andres Torres

Q90: This player led the Mets to victory against the Astros, 17-1. His line for the game: 6-for-6, six runs, one double, three home runs, and five RBIs. He's the only player in franchise history with six hits and three home runs in a single-game. Who achieved this once-in-a-lifetime fantastic feat?
   a) Yoenis Cespedes
   b) Wilmer Flores
   c) Howard Johnson
   d) Edgardo Alfonzo

TOP OF THE FIFTH ANSWER KEY

81: d. Moises Alou (2007).

82: c. Benny Agbayani/Edgardo Alfonzo (1999-2000).

83: a. John Olerud (1988-89).

84: c. Pete Alonso (2019).

85: c. Richard Hidalgo (2004).

86: a. David Wright (2008).

87: d. Mike Piazza (1999, 2000).

88: d. Yoenis Cespedes.

89: a. Scott Hairston.

90: d. Edgardo Alfonzo (1999).

BOTTOM OF THE FIFTH

Q91: Only one player in Mets history had multiple five-hit games in a single-season. To give you an idea how hard it is to get five hits in a game, the Mets had only five such games—by five different players—from 2015-19. Who had a franchise record *three* five-hit games in a single-season?
  a) Mike Piazza
  b) Dave Magadan
  c) Keith Hernandez
  d) Jose Reyes

Q92: Wins Above Replacement (WAR) is a metric that seeks to answer this question: How many wins does a player add to his team compared with what a replacement player would add? It can vary slightly due to the calculations of your preferred database, but it's one of the most robust measures of a player's contribution to team success. For example, using the Baseball-Reference metric for position players, Cody Bellinger led MLB with 9.0 WAR in 2019—and he won the NL MVP Award. Whose 8.3 WAR Position Player is the highest single-season total in Mets history?
  a) Pete Alonso
  b) David Wright
  c) Carlos Beltran
  d) Bernard Gilkey

Q93: Dave Kingman was the first player in Mets history with multiple 30-homer seasons. Pete Alonso might own this record one day—but for the moment, who is the only player in Mets history to achieve this fantastic feat four times?
  a) Darryl Strawberry

b) Howard Johnson
c) Mike Piazza
d) David Wright

Q94: Dave Kingman hit three home runs in a game on June 4, 1976—and he set a franchise single-game record with eight RBIs. That record would last more than four decades. Who broke Kingman's record with nine RBIs in a single-game?
a) Yoenis Cespedes
b) Carlos Delgado
c) Juan Lagares
d) Todd Frazier

Q95: A huge game is great … but multiple huge games? Outstanding. This player had 10 games for the Mets with five or more RBIs. That's a franchise record. Who achieved this fantastic feat?
a) Todd Hundley
b) Darryl Strawberry
c) David Wright
d) Mike Piazza

Q96: The modern definition of a "quality start" is six-plus innings while giving up three or fewer earned runs. The single-season franchise record for quality starts is 33—and it included 16 complete games. Who achieved this fantastic feat?
a) Dwight Gooden
b) Tom Seaver
c) David Cone
d) Jacob deGrom

Q97: And a follow-up … one pitcher made 26 consecutive quality

starts in a single-season. Who achieved this fantastic feat?
a) Dwight Gooden
b) Tom Seaver
c) David Cone
d) Jacob deGrom

Q98: The first regular season game at Citi Field was on April 13, 2009. Who homered that day for the Mets?
a) Daniel Murphy
b) Carlos Beltran
c) Jeff Francoeur
d) David Wright

Q99: This player was 21 years, 264 days old, when he hit an opposite-field, ninth-inning, game-winning home run on the road in Philadelphia. That made him the youngest Mets player since David Wright (21 years, 243 days) to hit a go-ahead homer in the ninth inning or later. Not only that, but it was also his first big league bomb. Who achieved this remarkable feat?
a) Ruben Tejada
b) Wilmer Flores
c) Dominic Smith
d) Amed Rosario

Q100: Pete Alonso's record-setting 2019 rookie campaign was the tenth season in Mets history in which a player had at least 30 home runs, 100 RBIs, and 100 runs scored. Prior to Alonso, who was the most recent Mets player to achieve this fantastic feat?
a) Carlos Beltran
b) David Wright
c) Mike Piazza
d) Bernard Gilkey

BOTTOM OF THE FIFTH ANSWER KEY

91: c. Keith Hernandez (1985).

92: b. David Wright (2007).

93: c. Mike Piazza. (1999-2002).

94: b. Carlos Delgado (2008).

95: c. David Wright.

96: a. Dwight Gooden (1985).

97: d. Jacob deGrom (2018).

98: d. David Wright.

99: d. Amed Rosario (August 11, 2017).

100: b. David Wright (2008).

"Words can't express it. I said it was a dream to win one [Cy Young Award], but to win back-to-back, honestly, I'm kind of speechless right now."

Jacob deGrom

6 AWARD WINNERS

Whitey Herzog famously said, "We need just two players to be a contender: Babe Ruth and Sandy Koufax."

It's a funny line.

It also underscores a significant truth: baseball is a team game. Even Herzog, in his jest, said *contender*. If you want to be a champion, then you need a team. You don't build a franchise as successful as the Mets unless the franchise culture embraces that simple fact.

But, the hardware *is* nice.

In the sixth, the trivia is all about award-winning Mets.

TOP OF THE SIXTH

Q101: This pitcher was the 2000 NLCS MVP as the Mets claimed their fourth NL pennant in franchise history. He was 2-0, and gave up just nine hits and no runs in 14 innings of work. He won Game One on the road, and he won the Game Five clincher at home. Who is this award-winning pitcher?
  a) Bobby Jones
  b) Al Leiter
  c) Rick Reed
  d) Mike Hampton

Q102: This player was the first in Mets history to win a batting title. He said afterward, "I'm humbled and honored. It's very special to be the first Mets player to win a batting title. There have been so many great players throughout our history." However, the title came with some controversy. He had a narrow lead in the batting title race as play began on the final day of the season—and when he singled in his first at-bat, he decided to come out of the game and take his chances that he had done enough to win. It was a home game, and fans who paid to see him play weren't happy … but, he's a batting champion. Who won this title?
  a) Lance Johnson
  b) Jose Reyes
  c) Carlos Beltran
  d) Carlos Delgado

Q103: Pete Alonso was the sixth player in franchise history to win Rookie of the Year honors. Who was the first?
  a) Tom Seaver
  b) Jon Matlack

c) Dave Kingman
d) Darryl Strawberry.

Q104: And a follow-up … Mets manager Mickey Callaway said of Pete Alonso: "He does everything the right way and he only cares about winning." Well, in addition to winning the 2019 NL Rookie of the Year Award, home run title, and Home Run Derby … how many times did Alonso win NL Rookie of the Month honors?
　a) 1
　b) 2
　c) 3
　d) 4

Q105: No player in Mets history has ever won league MVP honors … but the Cy Young Award is a different story. Jacob deGrom won his second Cy Young in 2019. How many times overall has a Mets pitcher won the Cy Young?
　a) 6
　b) 7
　c) 8
　d) 9

Q106: The first NL Player of the Week recipient in Mets history was a pitcher. He beat Houston with six innings of four-hit ball, and later that same week he pitched a complete game five-hit shutout vs. Atlanta. Who was the first Met to win a NL Player of the Week Award?
　a) Tom Seaver
　b) Jerry Koosman
　c) Jon Matlack
　d) Tug McGraw

Q107: In 2019, Pete Alonso became just the fourth player in Mets history to win the NL home run title. Who was the first?
   a) Darryl Strawberry
   b) Cleon Jones
   c) Dave Kingman
   d) Howard Johnson

Q108: This pitcher led the league with 10.1 Total WAR—and as a result, he also won the NL Cy Young Award. Who is this award-winning pitcher?
   a) R.A. Dickey
   b) Jacob deGrom
   c) Dwight Gooden
   d) Tom Seaver

Q109: The Roberto Clemente Award is one of the most prestigious in baseball. It is "given annually to a player who demonstrates the values Hall of Famer Roberto Clemente displayed in his commitment to community and understanding the value of helping others" (MLB.com). Mets players have won this award an astounding four times. Who was the first player in Mets history to receive this great honor?
   a) Gary Carter
   b) Ron Darling
   c) John Franco
   d) Ed Kranepool

Q110: And a follow-up … who was the most recent player to win the Roberto Clemente Award?
   a) David Wright
   b) Daniel Murphy
   c) Curtis Granderson

d) Tom Glavine

TOP OF THE SIXTH ANSWER KEY

101: d. Mike Hampton.

102: b. Jose Reyes (2011).

103: a. Tom Seaver (1967).

104: c. 3 (April, June, and September).

105: b. 7 (deGrom, 2; Tom Seaver, 3; Dwight Gooden, 1; R.A. Dickey, 1).

106: d. Tug McGraw (1974).

107: c. Dave Kingman (1982).

108: b. Jacob deGrom (2018).

109: a. Gary Carter (1989).

110: c. Curtis Granderson (2016).

BOTTOM OF THE SIXTH

Q111: Richie Ashburn was the first All-Star in Mets history. It was the inaugural 1962 season, and the last season of the veteran outfielder's career. Ashburn hit .306 with seven home runs that year. As for the All-Star Game, it was actually a two-game series in 1962. Ashburn sat the first game (the NL won, 3-1), but in the second game (the NL lost, 9-4) he came off the bench as a pinch-hitter and singled. He later scored on an RBI groundout by Dick Groat—which made Ashburn the first player in Mets history to get a hit and score a run in the Mid-Summer Classic. It was 1979 before a Mets player homered in the All-Star Game. Lee Mazzilli got his name in the record books for that one. However, in 40 years since Mazzilli went yard ... only one other Mets player has hit an All-Star Game home run: David Wright, in 2006. Wright played in seven All-Star Games, more than any other player in Mets history. Tom Seaver leads the way for pitchers—he was a nine-time All-Star for the Mets, and he appeared in six of those games. Only one player in Mets history has won All-Star Game MVP honors. Which pitcher achieved this feat?
 a) Dwight Gooden
 b) Tom Seaver
 c) Jon Matlack
 d) Pedro Martinez

Q112: The MLB Players Choice Awards are billed as "players honor their own" (MLB.com). The Players Choice Outstanding Pitcher Award was first given in 1994. Greg Maddux, who was with the Atlanta Braves at that time, was the NL recipient. Who was the first member of the Mets to win the Players Choice Outstanding Pitcher Award?

a) R.A. Dickey
b) Jacob deGrom
c) Al Leiter
d) Mike Hampton

Q113: Pete Alonso won the NL Players Choice Outstanding Rookie Award for 2019. He was the second Mets player to win this honor. Who was the first?
a) Jacob deGrom
b) David Wright
c) Ike Davis
d) Noah Syndergaard

Q114: The Pitching Triple Crown is when a pitcher leads his league in wins, strikeouts and ERA. Who is the only pitcher in Mets history to claim this honor?
a) Tom Seaver
b) Dwight Gooden
c) David Cone
d) Jerry Koosman

Q115: The Mets swept the Cubs in the 2015 NLCS to win the fifth pennant in franchise history. Who was the 2015 NLCS MVP after hitting four home runs vs. the Cubs?
a) Yoenis Cespedes
b) Lucas Duda
c) Travis d'Arnaud
d) Daniel Murphy

Q116: The Reliever of the Year Awards are now named after Trevor Hoffman and Mariano Rivera—the greatest all-time closers from each league. Who is the only Mets closer to win NL Reliever of the

Year?

a) Armando Benitez
b) Jeurys Familia
c) Francisco Rodriguez
d) Billy Wagner

Q117: The predecessor to the Reliever of the Year Award was called Fireman of the Year. It was an apt description of what relievers do—and this guy was one of the best ... who is the only two-time Fireman of the Year Award recipient in Mets history?

a) Jesse Orosco
b) Tug McGraw
c) Roger McDowell
d) John Franco

Q118: In 1983, Dwight Gooden was the first prospect in Mets history to win the *Baseball America* Minor League Player of the Year Award. Who is the only player in Mets history to win that same award ... *twice?*

a) Pete Alonso
b) Ike Davis
c) Gregg Jefferies
d) Darryl Strawberry

Q119: Only once in Mets history has a player won *Sports Illustrated* Sportsperson of the Year honors. Who achieved this historic feat?

a) Tom Seaver
b) Tug McGraw
c) Dwight Gooden
d) Ray Knight

Q120: No manager in Mets history has ever won a Manager of the

Year Award given by MLB. However, the AP is a different story. Who is the only manager in Mets history to win the Associated Press Manager of the Year Award?

a) Davey Johnson
b) Gil Hodges
c) Yogi Berra
d) Bobby Valentine

BOTTOM OF THE SIXTH ANSWER KEY

111: c. Jon Matlack (1975).

112: a. R.A. Dickey (2012).

113: a. Jacob deGrom (2014).

114: b. Dwight Gooden (1985).

115: d. Daniel Murphy.

116: a. Armando Benitez (2001).

117: d. John Franco (1990, 1994).

118: c. Gregg Jefferies (1986, 1987).

119: a. Tom Seaver (1969).

120: b. Gil Hodges (1969).

"I had to be a blue collar-type of player. I mean, I had to apply myself and do repetition and really work my craft. And that's what I did."

Mike Piazza

7 THE HITTERS

In the seventh, it's all about the hitters. These are the players who hit bombs. The guys who hit for average. The guys who hit in the clutch. Some do all three. Like these guys. One hit nine "late and close" home runs in a single-season, while the other hit grand slams in both ends of a doubleheader. Impressive, right?

How about walk-offs?
Check.
Walk-offs in the playoffs?
You bet.
Lead-off home runs?
Obviously.
Historic debuts?
Absolutely.
The list could go on, and on, and on.
Let's get started.

TOP OF THE SEVENTH

Q121: Win Probability Added (WPA) is an event-based stat, that measures "the importance of a given plate appearance in the context of the game" (MLB.com). If you hit a grand slam, it's pretty awesome—but if you hit it after your team already has a 10-run lead, then it's not worth nearly as much as a solo home run when your team is trailing by a run. Hence, the context factor. The actual measurement is the probability your at-bat adds to or detracts from your team's odds of winning an individual game. Whose career 30.164 WPA is the highest for any position player in Mets history?
   a) David Wright
   b) Darryl Strawberry
   c) Carlos Beltran
   d) Mike Piazza

Q122: To give more context, Christian Yelich led MLB with 7.1 WPA for the Brewers in 2019. The league MVPs—Mike Trout and Cody Bellinger—had 5.2 and 5.0, respectively. Who holds the Mets single-season record with 5.989 WPA?
   a) Carlos Beltran
   b) John Olerud
   c) Mike Piazza
   d) Bernard Gilkey

Q123: By definition a "late and close" situation is "the seventh inning or later with the hitter's team tied, ahead by one, or has the tying run on base, at bat, or on deck" (MLB.com). In other words, *clutch*. Who set a franchise single-season record with *nine* home runs in late and close situations?
   a) George Foster

b) Dave Kingman
c) Todd Hundley
d) Pete Alonso

Q124: And a follow-up ... who owns the career record with 36 late and close home runs for the Mets?
a) Howard Johnson
b) Darryl Strawberry
c) Mike Piazza
d) David Wright

Q125: Apply today's metrics to players from yesteryear, and this guy holds the franchise record with 267 career late and close hits. Literally, the guy held a record for decades ... but didn't know it, because the stat didn't exist in his time. Anyway, who gets credit in today's record books for the most late and close hits in Mets history?
a) Cleon Jones
b) Ed Kranepool
c) Jerry Grote
d) Bud Harrelson

Q126: Batting Average on Balls in Play (BABIP) excludes home runs, and instead measures how often a batted ball goes for a hit (FanGraphs.com). It can tell you if a player is successful (or not) due to talent, defense, or luck. The logic behind it suggests hitters have more control over batted ball outcomes than do pitchers. To give it more context, Yoan Moncada hit .315 with 25 home runs in 2019—but his .406 BABIP led all MLB. Among players who qualified for the batting title, who led the Mets with a .338 BABIP in 2019?
a) Amed Rosario
b) Jeff McNeil
c) Wilson Ramos

d) Michael Conforto

Q127: And a follow-up … who set a single-season franchise record with a .394 BABIP?
a) Roger Cedeno
b) John Olerud
c) David Wright
d) Rickey Henderson

Q128: Isolated Power (ISO) measures raw power as the ratio of extra bases per at-bat, and reveals how often a player hits for extra bases (FanGraphs.com). It better reflects the type of hitter you are evaluating than does traditional batting average or slugging percentage. For context, Mike Trout led MLB with .353 ISO in 2019—and he was the AL MVP. The Mets single-season record is .323 ISO. Who holds this record?
a) Pete Alonso
b) Carlos Beltran
c) Carlos Delgado
d) Mike Piazza

Q129: The single-season franchise record for extra-base hits is 85. That total led the league, and was third in MLB. Who holds this franchise record?
a) Howard Johnson
b) Todd Hundley
c) Pete Alonso
d) Bernard Gilkey

Q130: This slugger was the first player in major-league history to hit a grand slam in both games of a doubleheader. Who achieved this historic first?

a) Mike Piazza
b) Robin Ventura
c) Kevin McReynolds
d) Howard Johnson

TOP OF THE SEVENTH ANSWER KEY

121: a. David Wright.

122: b. John Olerud (1998).

123: d. Pete Alonso (2019).

124: a. Howard Johnson.

125: b. Ed Kranepool.

126: a. Amed Rosario.

127: c. David Wright (2009).

128: a. Pete Alonso (2019).

129: c. Pete Alonso (2019).

130: b. Robin Ventura (1999).

BOTTOM OF THE SEVENTH

Q131: Only 12 players in Mets history had at least one season with 100 or more runs scored. Who holds the single-season record with 127 runs scored?
 a) Lance Johnson
 b) Jose Reyes
 c) Carlos Beltran
 d) Edgardo Alfonzo

Q132: And a follow-up ... a handful of players had multiple seasons in which they scored at least 100 runs. Who is the only player in Mets history to score 100 or more runs in *four* different seasons?
 a) Lance Johnson
 b) Jose Reyes
 c) Carlos Beltran
 d) Edgardo Alfonzo

Q133: The most walk-off home runs by a player in Mets history is four. It's a record shared by a handful of players. Some you would expect—Mike Piazza, Kevin McReynolds—but others, well ... not so much. In parts of two seasons with the Mets, this player hit only 12 total home runs—but four of them were walk-offs, including two as a pinch-hitter. Who is the least likely member of the fraternity of players that share this record?
 a) Kelly Johnson
 b) Ryan Church
 c) Mike Jacobs
 d) Chris Jones

Q134: How about lead-off home runs? The highest career total in

Mets history is 21—shared by Jose Reyes and Curtis Granderson. However, the record for lead-off home runs as the *very* first batter of the game—as in, the top of the first—is 14. Who hit more lead-off home runs on the road than any player in Mets history?

a) Mookie Wilson
b) Lenny Dykstra
c) Jose Reyes
d) Curtis Granderson

Q135: This player was the first to hit a fair ball into the upper deck at Shea Stadium. His home run was so impressive, that it "was commemorated with a white circle painted into the facing of Section 48 at Shea Stadium" (MLB.com). Who hit this moonshot?

a) Dave Kingman
b) Tommie Agee
c) Mike Piazza
d) Darryl Strawberry

Q136: You often hear situational stats when watching a ballgame on TV or listening to one on the radio. Two outs with runners in scoring position is a big one. You can debate its usefulness as a stat … but either way, it's always going to be mentioned—especially when the game hangs in the balance. Among players with at least 200 career plate appearances with two outs and runners in scoring position, who hit a franchise best .361 (along with seven home runs and 84 RBIs)?

a) Dave Magadan
b) Kevin Mitchell
c) Daniel Murphy
d) John Olerud

Q137: And a follow-up … these teammates share a record set in the same season. Which duo each had 29 hits with two outs and runners

in scoring position during a single-season?
 a) Cleon Jones/Ken Boyer
 b) Jose Reyes/David Wright
 c) Mookie Wilson/Keith Hernandez
 d) Daniel Murphy/Marlon Byrd

Q138: The Mets had 96 batters combine to hit 181 grand slams from 1962 through 2019. Who hit a franchise best six career grand slams?
 a) Mike Piazza
 b) Robin Ventura
 c) Kevin McReynolds
 d) Carlos Beltran

Q139: This player hit a walk-off grand slam in the playoffs … but the celebration was so intense that he never finished his trip around the bases, so the official scoring on his hit was a single. Whose "grand slam single" would have been the first-ever walk-off grand slam in postseason history?
 a) Mike Piazza
 b) Robin Ventura
 c) Kevin McReynolds
 d) Carlos Beltran

Q140: Only one player in Mets history had three hits *and* a home run in his major-league debut. He was 3-for-3, with two doubles, a home run, one run scored, and three RBIs. He also walked twice—one of which was intentional. No other player this century—across all 30 MLB teams—has been perfect at the plate, with a home run and IBB in his major-league debut. Whose debut went into the record books?
 a) Nick Evans

b) Ike Davis
c) Lucas Duda
d) Kazuo Matsui

BOTTOM OF THE SEVENTH ANSWER KEY

131: c. Carlos Beltran (2006).

132: b. Jose Reyes.

133: d. Chris Jones.

134: d. Curtis Granderson.

135: b. Tommie Agee (1969).

136: d. John Olerud.

137: b. Jose Reyes/David Wright (2006).

138: a. Mike Piazza.

139: b. Robin Ventura (1999 NLCS Game Five vs. Atlanta Braves).

140: d. Kazuo Matsui (April 6, 2004).

"I figured that pitchers had a better chance of getting drafted than fielders, so I decided I should be a pitcher. But I never expected to be picked in the first-round. I wasn't even sure I'd get picked at all."

Dwight Gooden

8 THE PITCHERS

In the eighth, it's all about the pitchers. Guys who can paint the corners and throw gas. League leaders, franchise records, mind-blowing stats. One guy beat all 30 MLB teams, while another retired 25 in a row to start a game … and yet another made 33 consecutive scoreless appearances.

Cy Young winners?
Check.
Historic debuts?
Check.
Franchise records?
Check.
Let's get started.

TOP OF THE EIGHTH

Q141: Fielding Independent Pitching (FIP) is a number similar to ERA, however, "it focuses solely on the events a pitcher has the most control over: strikeouts, unintentional walks, hit-by-pitches, and home runs" (MLB.com). The idea is to eliminate results on balls in play, because a pitcher has no control over their outcome—and for that reason, FIP is often considered a better metric than ERA for determining a pitcher's effectiveness. For example, you can have a low FIP and a high ERA—which would indicate bad luck on balls in play, and a guy you don't want to give up on. If you apply FIP throughout Mets history … then who produced a franchise best 1.69 FIP for a single-season?
    a) Dwight Gooden
    b) Tom Seaver
    c) Jacob deGrom
    d) David Cone

Q142: And a follow-up … among pitchers with at least 500 innings, who has the lowest career FIP in Mets history?
    a) David Cone
    b) Tom Seaver
    c) Dwight Gooden
    d) Jacob deGrom

Q143: Wins Above Replacement (WAR)—this time for pitchers—adjusts FIP for factors such as league and ballpark, and then uses league averages to determine "how many wins a pitcher was worth based on those numbers and his innings pitched total" (MLB.com). Which pitcher has the highest career WAR in Mets history?
    a) David Cone

b) Tom Seaver
c) Dwight Gooden
d) Jacob deGrom

Q144: And a follow-up ... which pitcher had the highest single-season WAR in Mets history?
a) David Cone
b) Tom Seaver
c) Dwight Gooden
d) Jacob deGrom

Q145: Adjusted Earned Run Average (ERA+) normalizes a pitcher's ERA by accounting "for external factors like ballparks and opponents" (MLB.com). A score of 100 is the league average, so a score of 150 is 50% better than the league average. Among pitchers with 500 innings, whose career 147 ERA+ is the best all-time in Mets history?
a) David Cone
b) Tom Seaver
c) Dwight Gooden
d) Jacob deGrom

Q146: Tom Seaver is the franchise career leader with 198 wins. Seaver, Dwight Gooden, and Jerry Koosman are the only players to win more than 100 games for the Mets. A fourth pitcher came up one short. Who won exactly 99 games during nine seasons with the Mets?
a) Jon Matlack
b) Al Leiter
c) Sid Fernandez
d) Ron Darling

Q147: The Mets have never had a perfect game. This pitcher came the closest. He retired the first 25 batters he faced in a start vs. the Chicago Cubs, but gave up a single in the ninth. He had to settle for a one-hit shutout, with 11 strikeouts. Who came closer to perfection than any other pitcher in Mets history?
   a) Pedro Martinez
   b) Dwight Gooden
   c) Tom Seaver
   d) Sid Fernandez

Q148: This relief pitcher set a franchise record when he made 33 consecutive appearances in a single-season without giving up a run—earned or otherwise. He pitched 27 innings, gave up just 14 hits and nine walks, and struck out 26. Who set this record?
   a) Anthony Young
   b) Billy Wagner
   c) Jerry Blevins
   d) Mark Guthrie

Q149: This relief pitcher set a franchise record when he recorded a save in 14 consecutive appearances in a single-season. Who set this record?
   a) Armando Benitez
   b) Jeurys Familia
   c) John Franco
   d) Billy Wagner

Q150: This pitcher wrote his name in the history books with a victory over the Arizona Diamondbacks. It made him the first pitcher to defeat all 30 current MLB teams. Who achieved this historic first while pitching for the Mets?
   a) Mike Hampton

b) Al Leiter
c) Kevin Appier
d) Pedro Martinez

TOP OF THE EIGHTH ANSWER KEY

141: a. Dwight Gooden (1984).

142: b. Tom Seaver (2.67).

143: b. Tom Seaver (76.0).

144: c. Dwight Gooden (1985).

145: d. Jacob deGrom.

146: d. Ron Darling.

147: c. Tom Seaver (1969).

148: d. Mark Guthrie (2002).

149: b. Jeurys Familia (2016).

150: b. Al Leiter (2002).

BOTTOM OF THE EIGHTH

Q151: The Mets had a season in which the offense scored three or more runs in 23 of this pitcher's 35 starts. The club's record in those games was 22-1, and the pitcher's record was an astounding 19-0. There have been 60 times in franchise history in which the offense scored three or more runs for the same pitcher at least 23 times in a single-season—but only once did the pitcher post an unblemished record. Who achieved this extraordinary feat?
   a) David Cone
   b) Dwight Gooden
   c) Tom Seaver
   d) R.A. Dickey

Q152: Only eight closers in NL history had a season with 50-plus saves. Eric Gagne had back-to-back 50-save seasons with the Dodgers in 2002-03, and he remains the only NL pitcher to ever achieve that feat. The first pitcher in NL history to save 50 games in a single-season was Randy Myers. It was 1993, and Myers was pitching for the Chicago Cubs—but you might remember that he began his career with the Mets. There is one pitcher on that list of eight who saved 50 games for the Mets. In fact, he led the majors with 51 saves in 56 chances to set a franchise record. Whose name is in this record books for this feat?
   a) Billy Wagner
   b) John Franco
   c) Jeurys Familia
   d) Francisco Rodriguez

Q153: Six different closers had at least one 30-save season for the Mets. Four of those closers had multiple 30-save seasons. But only one of those four was able to achieve this remarkably consistent feat: He had 30 or more saves in three consecutive seasons. Whose name is in the record books for this one?

a) John Franco
b) Armando Benitez
c) Billy Wagner
d) Francisco Rodriguez

Q154: Only one pitcher in Mets history had double-digit strikeouts in his major-league debut. He beat Arizona, 3-1, gave up just three hits, and struck out 11 Diamondbacks in 5 1/3 innings. Whose name is in the record books for this one?

a) Jacob deGrom
b) Zack Wheeler
c) Matt Harvey
d) Steven Matz

Q155: And a follow-up … this pitcher had a historic major-league debut as well. He was 3-for-3 at the plate, with four RBIs. He also pitched 7 2/3 innings of five-hit ball to beat the Cincinnati Reds, 7-2. He's the only pitcher in Mets history with three hits or four RBIs—let alone both—in his big-league debut. Whose name is in the record books for this one?

a) Jacob deGrom
b) Zack Wheeler
c) Matt Harvey
d) Steven Matz

Q156: As noted earlier: Win Probability Added (WPA) is an event-based stat. "It doesn't tell you how well a player performed, it tells you how important their performance was" (FanGraphs.com). WPA can be used for pitchers or hitters. Whose career 43.7 WPA is the

highest for any pitcher in Mets history?
   a) Tom Seaver
   b) Dwight Gooden
   c) Jacob deGrom
   d) David Cone

Q157: And a follow-up ... who set the single-season franchise record for pitchers with 9.9 WPA?
   a) Tom Seaver
   b) Dwight Gooden
   c) Jacob deGrom
   d) David Cone

Q158: As noted earlier, Tom Seaver won a franchise record 198 games. Who holds the single-season record with 25 wins?
   a) David Cone
   b) Jerry Koosman
   c) Dwight Gooden
   d) Tom Seaver

Q159: This pitcher was the youngest in Mets history to earn a win. Whose name is in the record books for this feat?
   a) Dwight Gooden
   b) Jim Bethke
   c) Bill Hepler
   d) Tug McGraw

Q160: Only one pitcher in Mets history had a season in which he tossed at least 11 complete games while giving up five or fewer hits. Who was this nearly unhittable innings-eating machine?
   a) Dwight Gooden
   b) Tom Seaver

c) Jerry Koosman
d) David Cone

BOTTOM OF THE EIGHTH ANSWER KEY

151: b. Dwight Gooden (1985).

152: c. Jeurys Familia (2016).

153: b. Armando Benitez (2000-02).

154: c. Matt Harvey (July 26, 2012).

155: d. Steven Matz (June 28, 2015).

156: a. Tom Seaver.

157: b. Dwight Gooden (1985).

158: d. Tom Seaver (1969).

159: b. Jim Bethke (18 years, 161 days; 1965).

160: b. Tom Seaver (1969).

"In baseball, my theory is to strive for consistency, not to worry about the numbers. If you dwell on statistics you get shortsighted. If you aim for consistency, the numbers will be there at the end."

Tom Seaver

9 THE TEAMS

As we move to the ninth, we take a look at some of the greatest players and moments in Mets history through the lens of *teams*. An opponent, year, or even a college—the answers are team-centered: From the first game in franchise history through the record-setting power of Pete Alonso and the 2019 Mets.

Close games?

Blowouts?

Dubious team feats?

Extraordinary milestones?

All here in the ninth. Let's get started.

TOP OF THE NINTH

Q161: Ron Darling played collegiately in the Ivy League. Darling and future Mets teammate Frank Viola—who played collegiately for St. Johns University—dueled once for 11 scoreless innings before St. Johns finally prevailed in the 12th. For which prestigious Ivy League school did Darling play college baseball?
   a) Harvard
   b) Yale
   c) Princeton
   d) Dartmouth

Q162: Ron Hunt was the first player in Mets history to start an All-Star Game … and he did so in the only All-Star Game to ever be played at Shea Stadium. Hunt was 1-for-3, and the NL won the game, 7-4, when Johnny Callison hit the third All-Star walk-off home run in MLB history. In which season was the All-Star Game played at Shea Stadium?
   a) 1964
   b) 1965
   c) 1966
   d) 1967

Q163: Tom Seaver was originally drafted by Atlanta … however, Seaver's collegiate season began before he agreed to terms with the Braves, which, at that time, violated a rule that stated "a player can't be signed off a college campus once his team has started playing." As a result, baseball commissioner William Eckert voided his contract and $40,000 signing bonus and a lottery was held for teams willing to match the Braves' original offer. Cleveland, Philadelphia, and New York matched the offer … but the Mets won the lottery. For which

school did Seaver play collegiately?
 a) Arizona State
 b) UCLA
 c) Pepperdine
 d) USC

Q164: The first official game in Mets history was April 11, 1962. It was a loss to the Cardinals in St. Louis, 11-4. The Mets played home games at the Polo Grounds for 1962-63, and lost both home openers. The Mets lost the final game played at the Polo Grounds as well. The first game at Shea Stadium? A loss, 4-3, to the Pirates. You might have noticed a trend. The Mets lost, a lot. In which season did the Mets finally win a home opener for the first time in franchise history?
 a) 1968
 b) 1969
 c) 1970
 d) 1971

Q165: Yankee Stadium was renovated in the 1970s, which meant the Yankees played home games at Shea Stadium for a spell. The Mets and the New York Jets of the NFL already called Shea home … and then added to that mix were the New York Giants, who called Shea home while Giants Stadium was under construction. All four teams played their home games at Shea Stadium in one calendar year … which was?
 a) 1973
 b) 1974
 c) 1975
 d) 1976

Q166: In April 2019, Forbes valued the New York Mets at $2.3 billion—the sixth highest valued team in MLB. In which year did an

investment group led by Nelson Doubleday and current owner Fred Wilpon purchase the Mets for an estimated $21.1 million?
- a) 1978
- b) 1979
- c) 1980
- d) 1981

Q167: The 1986 Mets won a franchise record 108 regular season games—and 27 of those games were blowouts, which is defined as winning by five or more runs. In which season did the Mets win a franchise record 34 games by five or more runs?
- a) 1988
- b) 1990
- c) 2006
- d) 2015

Q168: And a follow-up … the 1986 Mets won 29 one-run games. But that total isn't even among the top ten in franchise history. In which season did the Mets win a franchise record 41 games by a single-run?
- a) 1985
- b) 1969
- c) 1973
- d) 2006

Q169: And another follow-up … the 1986 Mets won eight games with walk-offs. If that number is less than you expected, take it as evidence that the offense and starting rotation were really, really good that year. In which season did the Mets set a franchise record with 14 walk-offs?
- a) 1969
- b) 1971

c) 2006

d) 2015

Q170: The Mets are 208-194 all-time vs. the American League since interleague play began in 1997. Which American League team did the Mets host in the first-ever interleague game at Shea Stadium?

a) Chicago White Sox

b) Boston Red Sox

c) Toronto Blue Jays

d) Texas Rangers

TOP OF THE NINTH ANSWER KEY

161: b. Yale.

162: a. 1964.

163: d. USC.

164: a. 1968.

165: c. 1975.

166: c. 1980.

167: c. 2006.

168: b. 1969.

169: b. 1971.

170: b. Boston Red Sox.

BOTTOM OF THE NINTH

Q171: The first wild-card berth in franchise history was 1999, but it took a wild finish—literally—to earn it. The Mets beat the Pittsburgh Pirates on a ninth-inning walk-off wild pitch ... on the final day of the regular season, to force a one-game playoff to decide the NL wild-card. Which team did the Mets beat in that one-game playoff to win the 1999 NL wild-card?
  a) Philadelphia Phillies
  b) Cincinnati Reds
  c) San Francisco Giants
  d) St. Louis Cardinals

Q172: The Mets and Yankees played a unique day-night doubleheader thanks to a rainout the previous month. The afternoon game was at Shea, while the night game was in the Bronx. In which season did the Mets and Yankees play a home and away on the same day?
  a) 1998
  b) 1999
  c) 2000
  d) 2001

Q173: Not every team can be historic in a good way. Sometimes historic feats are the embarrassing kind. The Mets had a team that went 0-13 at Shea Stadium for the month of August. It was just the third time in major-league history that a team was winless at home for an entire calendar month. And worse ... the skid continued in September, and all total the club lost a NL record 15 consecutive games at home. In which season did this nightmare streak occur?
  a) 1983

b) 1991
c) 2002
d) 2004

Q174: Hall of Famers Tom Glavine and Pedro Martinez both achieved significant milestones while pitching for the Mets. Glavine won his 300th game, and a month later Martinez struck out his 3,000th batter. In which season did Mets fans witness these historic achievements?
    a) 2006
    b) 2007
    c) 2008
    d) 2009

Q175: Citi Field hosted its first-ever game on March 29, 2009. It was a collegiate game that featured St. John's and Georgetown. A few days later the Mets played their first exhibition game in the new ballpark. Against which team did the Mets play the first-ever major-league game at Citi Field?
    a) New York Yankees
    b) Atlanta Braves
    c) Boston Red Sox
    d) Philadelphia Phillies

Q176: The Mets won a wild-card berth in 2016, after losing the 2015 World Series to the Kansas City Royals. It was just the second time in franchise history that the Mets made the playoffs in consecutive seasons—and it was the first time the Mets played in the Wild Card Game. Citi Field hosted, but the Mets lost. Who beat the Mets in the 2016 Wild Card Game?
    a) Los Angeles Dodgers
    b) St. Louis Cardinals

c) San Francisco Giants

d) Washington Nationals

Q177: The Mets selected Pete Alonso in the second-round of the 2016 Amateur Draft. For which university did Alonso star collegiately?

a) FSU

b) University of Miami

c) University of Florida

d) University of Central Florida

Q178: As noted earlier, Jacob deGrom began his collegiate career as a shortstop. For which university did deGrom star collegiately?

a) University of Tampa

b) Stetson University

c) University of South Florida

d) University of Central Florida

Q179: This club was playoff bound in mid-September, but then the wheels came off. The Mets lost the division lead, but still had a two-game lead in the wild-card chase with seven games left on the schedule. By the season's final day the wild-card chase was tied. It was going to be the Brewers or the Mets … and the Brewers beat the Cubs, while the Mets lost at home to the Marlins. In which season did fans suffer this whirlwind of disappointment?

a) 2007

b) 2014

c) 2008

d) 2005

Q180: Probably one of the longest off-seasons for fans to endure was after this club blew a seven-game lead with just 17 games left on the schedule. The Mets had two separate five-game losing streaks in the last two-and-a-half weeks, and lost at home to the Marlins on the season's final day when a victory would have forced a playoff game for the division title. In which season did this tragic collapse unfold?

a) 2007
b) 2014
c) 2008
d) 2005

BOTTOM OF THE NINTH ANSWER KEY

171: b. Cincinnati Reds.

172: c. 2000.

173: c. 2002.

174: b. 2007.

175: c. Boston Red Sox.

176: c. San Francisco Giants.

177: c. University of Florida.

178: b. Stetson University.

179: c. 2008 (the Phillies won the division title).

180: a. 2007 (the Phillies won the division title).

"I've had nine knee surgeries. I've had a couple of broken thumbs, one on each hand. I can look back at it and say it's worth it to be enshrined in Cooperstown. I don't have any pain in my knees right now."

Gary Carter

10 EXTRA INNINGS

There is no clock in baseball. You have to get 27 outs, and then you can go home. That's why you never leave a game early. You just don't know what's going to happen next.

But sometimes 27 outs aren't enough.

It's free baseball, and it could go all night. Tense. Exhilarating. And conventional wisdom is tossed. Everything is on the table, because all it takes to win is a single run.

That's why here in extras we've got a bit of everything trivia-wise: dominant closers, historic no-hitters, series clinching walk-offs, rookie superstars, clutch veterans …

Finish strong.

TOP OF THE TENTH

Q181: Total Zone Runs (TZR) is a Baseball-Reference metric used to measure total fielding runs above average, based on the number of plays made (Baseball-Reference.com). In short, it attempts to quantify how many runs a player saved or gave up in the field. It's been a decade since the Mets had a defender who ranked among the top 10 in baseball in this category. Who was the most recent to do so?
 a) Angel Pagan
 b) Jeff Francoeur
 c) Jason Bay
 d) Jose Reyes

Q182: Only five players in National League history had a season with 125 or fewer base hits … and 100 or more RBIs. It's tough to do, obviously—and you would assume a ton of home runs among those hits. However, this player had a season with 125 hits, 105 RBIs, and just 24 home runs. Who was historically productive with his 125 hits for the Mets?
 a) David Wright
 b) Gary Carter
 c) Mike Piazza
 d) Edgardo Alfonzo

Q183: It took more than 8,000 games to get the first no-hitter in franchise history. Long-term, people have questioned whether the 134 pitches he took to get 27 outs might have been too high a price to pay for the magical night … and after the game, manager Terry Collins said, "I'm very excited for him, but in five days, if his arm is bothering him, I'm not going to feel very good … I just couldn't take him out." Who beat the St. Louis Cardinals, 8-0, for the first no-

hitter in franchise history?
a) R.A. Dickey
b) Jon Niese
c) Johan Santana
d) Chris Young

Q184: And a follow-up ... every no-hitter has at least one crucial play. In this case, there were two. In the seventh inning, Mike Baxter, who grew up just down the street from Shea Stadium, made a running catch on the warning track to rob Yadier Molina. Baxter slammed into the wall on a dead sprint, and collapsed to the ground as team trainers rushed out to left field. R.A. Dickey said after the game, "That ball that Baxter caught, he'll go down in the annals of New York Mets lore because of that." The other crucial play: Umpire Adrian Johnson missed a call. In the sixth inning, this player hit a rocket down the third-base line, and replays show it hit the white chalk. But there were no replays in baseball at that time, and Johnson ruled it a foul ball. Who hit the ball that should've ruined the first no-hitter in Mets history?
a) David Freese
b) Matt Holliday
c) Carlos Beltran
d) Allen Craig

Q185: This pitcher appeared in a major-league record 1,252 games—including 372 with the Mets. Who holds this record?
a) John Franco
b) Randy Myers
c) Billy Wagner
d) Jesse Orosco

Q186: This player was the first in Mets history to clinch a playoff

series with a walk-off home run. Ironically, it was also his only hit of the series. Whose name is in the history books for this one?
   a) Darryl Hamilton
   b) Todd Pratt
   c) Lenny Dykstra
   d) Benny Agbayani

Q187: This player hit a grand slam for his first major-league home run. At 20 years and four days, he was the youngest player in more than four decades to hit a grand slam—and just two months later he became the youngest player ever to hit home runs from both sides of the plate in the same game. Who achieved these remarkable feats?
   a) Gregg Jefferies
   b) Mookie Wilson
   c) Lee Mazzilli
   d) Jose Reyes

Q188: Exit velocity "measures the speed of a baseball as it comes off the bat, immediately after a batter makes contact" (MLB.com). It can be used to evaluate hitters and pitchers. A high exit velocity increases the odds that a Batted Ball Event (BBE) will be positive—for the hitter, not so much if you're the pitcher. The highest exit velocity of 2019 came off the bat of Giancarlo Stanton—120.6 mph. How far did it go? Well, 279 feet. As singles go, that's not bad. The highest exit velocity for the Mets in 2019 was actually 118.3 mph. Who had the highest exit velocity of the season for the Mets?
   a) Pete Alonso
   b) J.D. Davis
   c) Robinson Cano
   d) Amed Rosario

Q189: And a follow-up … who led the 2019 Mets with an average

exit velocity of 91.4 mph?
- a) Pete Alonso
- b) J.D. Davis
- c) Robinson Cano
- d) Amed Rosario

Q190: For all the sluggers who have suited up for the Mets, only one has ever led the league in RBIs. Who achieved this feat?
- a) Mike Piazza
- b) Darryl Strawberry
- c) Howard Johnson
- d) Bernard Gilkey

TOP OF THE TENTH ANSWER KEY

181: a. Angel Pagan (2010, 19 TZR).

182: b. Gary Carter (1986).

183: c. Johan Santana (2012).

184: c. Carlos Beltran.

185: d. Jesse Orosco.

186: b. Todd Pratt (1999 NLDS vs. Arizona Diamondbacks).

187: d. Jose Reyes (2003).

188: a. Pete Alonso.

189: b. J.D. Davis.

190: c. Howard Johnson (117 RBIs, 1991).

BOTTOM OF THE TENTH

Q191: The 2015 Mets were shutout an astounding 15 times. Whose acquisition at the trade deadline turned the offense around and propelled the Mets to the fifth pennant in franchise history?
  a) Michael Cuddyer
  b) Yoenis Cespedes
  c) Curtis Granderson
  d) Kelly Johnson

Q192: In 2016, 42-year-old pitcher Bartolo Colon hit his first major-league home run. That easily makes him the oldest player in franchise history at the time of his first career home run ... but who is the *oldest* player to ever hit a home run for the Mets?
  a) Willie Mays
  b) Moises Alou
  c) Gary Sheffield
  d) Julio Franco

Q193: In 2018, Jacob deGrom had a 1.69 ERA through his first 16 starts. Only once in Mets history did a pitcher post a lower ERA in his first 16 starts of a season. Who achieved this feat?
  a) Tom Seaver
  b) David Cone
  c) Dwight Gooden
  d) Pedro Martinez

Q194: This pitcher was the first in major-league history—not just for the Mets, but for any team, in any league—to strikeout 13 batters *and* hit a home run in the same game ... *twice*. Whose name is in the MLB record book for this historic feat?

a) Dwight Gooden
b) Tom Seaver
c) Jacob deGrom
d) Jerry Koosman

Q195: This rookie was the first in major-league history with 11 extra-base hits during his first 10 career games. Whose name is in the record books for this feat?
a) Mike Jacobs
b) Benny Agbayani
c) Darryl Strawberry
d) Pete Alonso

Q196: This pitcher tossed a complete game shutout *and* hit a home run in the same game … and the final was 1-0. He's the only pitcher in Mets history to combine those feats into a single-game. Who pitched and slugged his way into the record books?
a) Jacob deGrom
b) Tom Seaver
c) Dwight Gooden
d) Noah Syndergaard

Q197: This pitcher was the first in baseball's modern era—since 1900—to win his first three starts of a season, while striking out at least 25 batters and giving up six or fewer total hits. Who achieved this remarkable feat?
a) Nolan Ryan
b) Matt Harvey
c) Sid Fernandez
d) Noah Syndergaard

Q198: This pitcher is the only one in Mets history to throw nine

innings, give up just one hit and no walks, strikeout 12 batters ... and get a no-decision. Whose name is in the record books for this feat?
a) Nolan Ryan
b) Matt Harvey
c) Sid Fernandez
d) Noah Syndergaard

Q199: The final game at Shea Stadium was on September 28, 2008. Who was on the mound for the ceremonial first pitch?
a) Mike Piazza
b) Tom Seaver
c) Jerry Koosman
d) Davey Johnson

Q200: The Mets retired the name "Shea" on April 8, 2008, as the club began its 45th and final season at Shea Stadium. A fan vote was held that season to select the Top 10 Moments in Shea Stadium History. Which moment was voted #1 by the fans?
a) Game Six of the 1986 World Series
b) Mike Piazza's home run in NYC's first game after 9/11
c) Game Five of the 1969 World Series
d) Tom Seaver's near perfect game

BOTTOM OF THE TENTH ANSWER KEY

191: b. Yoenis Cespedes.

192: d. Julio Franco (48 years, 254 days).

193: c. Dwight Gooden (1.68 ERA, 1985).

194: c. Jacob deGrom (2019).

195: d. Pete Alonso (2019).

196: d. Noah Syndergaard (2019).

197: b. Matt Harvey (2013).

198: b. Matt Harvey (2013).

199: b. Tom Seaver.

200: a. Game Six of the 1986 World Series.

ABOUT THE AUTHOR

Tucker Elliot is a former teacher, coach, and athletic director. He has visited schools on four continents and more than twenty countries as a volunteer or an invited speaker/lecturer. He lives in Florida and Korea.

e-Books by Tucker Elliot

The Day Before 9/11

The Memory of Hope

The Rainy Season

Third Ring Children

The Other Side of the River

Baseball Books by Tucker Elliot

Los Angeles Dodgers IQ: The Ultimate Test of True Fandom

Baltimore Orioles IQ: The Ultimate Test of True Fandom

Cincinnati Reds IQ: The Ultimate Test of True Fandom

Major League Baseball IQ: The Ultimate Test of True Fandom

Tampa Bay Rays IQ: The Ultimate Test of True Fandom

Atlanta Braves IQ: The Ultimate Test of True Fandom

Cleveland Indians IQ: The Ultimate Test of True Fandom

Houston Astros IQ: The Ultimate Test of True Fandom

New York Yankees IQ: The Ultimate Test of True Fandom

San Francisco Giants IQ: The Ultimate Test of True Fandom

Washington Nationals IQ: The Ultimate Test of True Fandom

Atlanta Braves: An Interactive Guide to the World of Sports

Boston Red Sox: An Interactive Guide to the World of Sports

San Francisco Giants: An Interactive Guide to the World of Sports

51 Questions for the Diehard Fan: New York Yankees

51 Questions for the Diehard Fan: Atlanta Braves

51 Questions for the Diehard Fan: Baltimore Orioles

BLACK MESA

Visit us on the web to learn more:

www.blackmesabooks.com

SOURCES

Baseball-Reference.com (Play Index)

FanGraphs.com

MLB.com (and the official team sites through MLB.com)

BaseballHallofFame.org

ESPN.com

SABR.org

Baseball-Almanac.com

Elias Sports Bureau

www.ingramcontent.com/pod-product-compliance
Lightning Source LLC
Chambersburg PA
CBHW061445040426
42450CB00007B/1224